GW01311583

SARAH NEWTON

WE LOVE TO GROW

Empowering, restorative ideas to get you started growing edible plants in small urban spaces sustainably.

First edition

This book was professionally typeset on Reedsy.
Find out more at reedsy.com

To everyone and everything that have ever inspired me to connect to my environment and enjoyment of it, and to those who will continue to do so; what goes around comes around. With love.

Those who dwell among the beauties and mysteries of the Earth are never alone or weary of life.

Rachel Carson

Contents

1

Why I got into growing in small spaces

I got really into growing in small spaces when I moved into a 3rd storey Art Deco flat with my friend Parky. We both had a few crazy succulent house plants, and I'd just signed up for courses in Horticulture and Garden Design and had started working for a landscaping company. I was obsessed with plants. I wanted to learn more about all of them; how they grew, how to grow them as close to nature as possible, organically as possible, (I didn't want to use chemicals as I had become skin sensitive to a lot of chemicals and took that as a message that maybe I could do without inflicting too many processed chemicals on myself or my environment), what other plants the plants liked, what plants people liked, and how I could grow in synergizing these growing understandings. As I stood on the balcony and looked wistfully through the trees at the huge allotment site below I knew I couldn't wait until I got a plot there to get stuck in. It wasn't long till the flat and balcony and top of the rear stairs were full of plants, and I was well on my way to experimenting with growing various edibles in this mix. I knew this would be a lifelong interest, as there is always something new and exciting to learn and enjoy. Now I hope to share some part of my enjoyment and journey into extending possibilities of learning with you, and encourage you to experiment and grow and share what you find.

Photo by Zoe Schaeffer on Unsplash

2

Good ground rules and principles of Regenerative gardening, Urban Ecology; how we can all do it. And what it isn't. Oh and a bit of History and creative takes

Ok so we've all heard of Organic gardening, and growing locally, and how these terms can be undermined. One thing we humans really like to do is come up with a concept, then push it to the max, so we can capitalise on our 'idea'. It is especially marked as a process in our confusing modernity and complex choices.

Photo by Dan Cristian Pădureț on Unsplash

We can find organically grown vegetables on our supermarket shelves and in our markets that were grown in monoculture desert and flown a very long way from point of origination, (who doesn't like edamame, or almonds or avocados), or and in some cases grown in land that surely had more global and diverse value in being tropical rainforest. So food miles, which is a subject in itself and not a simple one, is not the only anomaly.

Photo by Somi Jaiswal on Unsplash

We can also find 'Organically' grown vegetables and fruit that have begun their lives as plants shipped in from elsewhere, then planted in fields too large to sustain any bio diverse hedges and wild edges, with soils being washed away by the rains and not held in place.

In the beginnings of experiments leading into agriculture some estimated 12,000 - 23,000 years ago, and right through our development of 'the village' to 'the city' - the oldest city known at this time being Ur, a Sumerian city state built around 3800 BC and beyond, food storage and sharing as a resource was and has always been central to the design of how we lived.

N
1
2
3
4
5
6
7
8
9
10
11
12
13
14
15
16
17
18
19
20
21
22
23
24
25
26
0 10 50 100 200 (m)

(1). Plan of Ur.

The new general plan of Ur (drawn up by F. Ghio): 1: City Wall; 2: North Harbour; 3: Palace of Ennigaldi-Nanna; 4: Harbour Temple; 5: Houses on City Wall; 6: Kassite Fort; 7: enclosure of the Sacred Area in the neo-Babylonian period; 8: enclosure of the Sacred Area during the 3rd Dynasty; 9: Nanna Court; 10: Etemenniguru; 11: Ziggurat; 12: Nanna Temple; 13: Boat Shrine; 14: Ningal Temple; 15: Giparku; 16: Edublamakh; 17: Ganunmakh; 18: Ekhursag; 19: Mausolea of the 3rd Dynasty; 20: Royal Graves; 21: Nimintabba Temple; 22: Houses (EM District); 23: West Harbour; 24: Houses (AH District); 25: neo-Babylonian Houses; 26: Enki Temple

The sacred spaces became pivotal points for us as a species. It was where we gathered to give and receive gifts of food, ideas, political power and ideology. We were bonded to our communities through this complex web as farmers, makers, hunters, leaders, families.

Market exchanges. Photo by Markus Spiske on Unsplash

As we have evolved and travelled as a species, so have our food plants, our textiles, crafts, precious resources of all kinds, and our means of transport, growth, trade complexities. But we can still see today even by looking at our cities, the importance of access to a simple central point for distribution through sales at the Markets.

London like many cities has many remnants of street names that hint to their previous use. One example, 'Fish Hill' at the top end used to join up to a huge Fish Market, only a few streets away from the Thames, named 'West Fish Market', which was known for its purpose at least from Mediaeval times.

(2) Horwood's 1799 map 'Fish Street'
(London's Alleys: Old Fish Street Hill, EC4, 2022)

Croydon has the remnant market on a street that under lots of names such as Butcherie and Butcher Row has been a Market since records of 1236.

We are becoming aware that there are many Urban spaces which need us to become re-empowered in the way we use and re-use them. Many cities are built on old cities and landfill, and have little green space to lower temperature within these spaces, or allow water back to feed green spaces, or imbue a sense of pride, belonging and connection.

By allowing spaces to be re-greened in a multi layered and meaningful way we can add back a whole appreciation and love of space and identity, ecology, stability and future enjoyment and use.

Ecology is a global issue and so is Environmentalism. We all need to eat, sleep, and live. We can do this better with a little initiative, creativity and belief.

We can create Sanctuary. We can grow edible plants in small spaces and love it. It is a joy to engage in this. Here are some great examples;

Photo by Jonathan Kemper on Unsplash

In 1991 when Cuba had a 'Special period' and its inhabitants experienced a huge economic crash, the only answer to enable surviving and thriving was to restore a whole lot of growing asap. Cubans deployed soil conservation techniques, biopesticides, worm compost, (vermiculture). Organic gardening was a keystone. The Organoponico - the small farm - was central to this. (3.) This was happening in the cities as much as in the wider agricultural domain. Fuel was so expensive that people were encouraged to use Ox to move the plough. This push was born out of need as chemicals were too expensive and people needed to be fed. The results were amazing and well publicised. People were able to survive and thrive better. Less monocultural sugar was being grown for export, less chemicals being added into the soil. Then 2020 also brought a similar slowing of imports and exports held in very few hands both inside and outside the Country with political complexities that forced a fresh re-focus upon agro ecology and restorative practices. People again simply didn't have enough food to eat.

The squeeze on flow of resources caused by political and corporate bodies, poorer monocrop harvest due to harsher climate, slower tourism and increasing prices are now becoming experienced and understood by more of us across the globe. We can all understand what it might mean, to varying degrees of our own experience. The fact that soil degradation caused by overworking, pollution, climate stresses and unsustainable techniques still exist in Cuba and every Country in the World shows us we have work to do. Regeneration can be for a whole benefit.

(4.) Cuba and others like her have taken on the notion of *agrihood* which was a term trademarked by a Development Company in Southern California in 2014, designing working farms as pivotal to planned

Communities, and from middle to very high end. These now number 90 or more in the USA, and as a response to a design need it is interesting. This notion has now been augmented by another take on this idea from a different viewpoint, and equally valid, although more so in its' ability to add value for all.

The Michigan Initiative is a 3 acre farm where Community are able to volunteer, and then benefit by a once a week harvest. Nutrition, and food security are but two of the output points. People get to make the produce into products like chilli sauce to share or sell.

Who doesn't like chilli sauce?

Photo by Albert Vincent Wu on Unsplash

The local economics and Community all win. Food sovereignty can be for all.

(5). Chicago also has amazing Community gardens. One in particular is in its 12th year. Harambee Garden rents plots to tenants for a very low rate but which covers the tools and materials needed to make and maintain the grow beds on what was a vacant lot, and the tenants get to keep or give away the food they grow. The initiative was born from a foundation of community volunteering and coming together under 'Root Riot' , Co - founded by Seamus Ford who grew up in the neighbourhood, with the vision of re deploying the many vacant lots "one planting bed at a time"', again with a huge impact on re empowering Community from the inside out.

The parallel to this in the UK, and variously across Europe, would be the 'allotment', found in Urban and rural situations since 1887, when the Allotments act made it necessary for local

Scaffold board pile intending for raised beds at allotments

authorities to provide plots where there was a request for them. This was a culmination point forced by the 'enclosures' of 1600's slowly forcing communities from sharing land openly.

Some are partially or wholly Community run and others are run by the community, with tenants, who again get to decide whether they use the food themselves or share it. Some sites have seed swaps, and lend tools, and most have access to water and allow some form of tool storage as sheds or tool boxes.

Local stables and tree surgeons often donate their horse manure and wood chippings to sites, and sometimes even a scaffold company might donate used scaff boards for repurposing as raised bed borders.

We have a history of Guerilla Gardening ever since lands became enclosed in the 1600's. The 'Diggers' were the first. Always for fun, usually to benefit the passerby and quite often to make a statement about the need to repurpose land and the concept of guardianship. Cities across the world are a hotbed for it.

Guerilla Garden logo amongst the strawberries by pixeltoo

There are also grassroots seed swaps, like 'Seedy Sunday' which has lasted 20 years, and mini charities and businesses focussed on seed sharing and knowledge sharing on a local basis.

Seedy Sunday seed packets for exchange or purchase.

Restorative gardening can be Organic, and local. It is a new phrase, as is needed by us now to reclaim the idea that food can be restorative on many levels, and not just a commodity to ship in. Urban Ecology is by some talked up as being contrary to 'Restorative gardening', as restoration in its most basic sense is to restore back to how it used to be. Urban Ecology is seen as a lens to study the services to Ecology and relieve the stresses within the environment as naturally reestablished in reclaimed environments.

Urban Ecology and Restoration gardening and agriculture as concepts can and should be co - workers and considered as the basis for developing new ways of valuing our developed and agricultural spaces, as well as giving space back for rewilding especially in the light of climate change and clear requirements by landscape in it's support of us and the wider Environment and species.

What if we all develop co-ownership through relationships with 'restoration/regenerative' gardening and 'Urban Ecology.' What do you think they can be to you? What kind of relationship would you like with them in your environment? Don't get caught up in exacting what other people think these words mean; maybe there isn't a right and wrong here; what can you enjoy in your environment as your starting point is enough to begin.

We can do this starting at home on our windowsills. It really is one step followed by another.

Photo by Kate Laine on Unsplash

3

Getting Started

Action steps

- Make a list of what edible plants you want to grow
- Consider nurturing some herbs and edible flowers in the mix if you can
- Do you know if they are Annuals/Perennials/Permanent plants? Make 3 lists and start putting those plants under the 3 headings, to help figure out what you need to plan for.
- Do you have a theme or a multi theme you want to embrace? Tropical meets Country garden for instance? Wetlands meet Desert, Or Purple meets Orange and white as a strict palette. Really a theme choice is fun and can be whatever you want it to be; recycled/upcycled/Tropical wonderland…. Set up a scrap book or page on the wall or a Pinterest page to collect ideas that are inspiring you.
- Look at your space. Watch it for the day in the season you are in. Where is the sun during the day? Are you south facing? Do a rough sketch of this space with symbols to remind yourself where the sunniest and shadiest places are. Also notice if any roof

lines stop water from falling directly below. These are called rain shadows. This means that if anything is planted below, some kind of adaptation to allow the water to access any planters would be helpful. Creativity may well be the mother of invention here; map it out. Taking pleasure and noticing the details of your growing space can bring great insights and ideas and fun! Try simple sketching or listing or words however you feel suits your own needs and personality.

Photo by KOBU Agency on Unsplash

- Planting for wildlife; have you considered which pollinators/ predators you want to attract and how?

- If you are going to make a growing space it is worth considering how needy your plants might be. Some are much more tolerant and hardy than others. What can you make moments for?
- It is worth considering a budget for each season and how costs might be shared or met. For instance, there are seed swaps in Springtime, and other local gardeners might like to share resources if you are on a shoestring.
- Plan on some fun resource /fact finding on your own or with family and friends.
- Plan on sharing and swapping your abundance, and ideas with friends, family and new people to you on a new network you will find. There is a wealth in this. Sharing memories and skills attached to how we have enjoyed plants and foods in cultural and familial terms is a great source of inspiration and wonderful to share.
- What part of regenerative gardening and or Urban Ecology really inspires you and how do you feel like celebrating and engaging these ideas for yourself?
- If you have access to ground or /and raw materials to mulch how will you be adding to the soil to make it healthier and build it further.

Photo by Gabriel Jimenez on Unsplash

4

How to grow well; main plant requirements, principles and definitions

So a basic list of things we have to take care of and consider to grow well;

- Containers to grow in that will be big enough to cater for your plant in the short term, (if it is a perennial it will grow larger each year, so will want a bigger space each year too unless you divide or prune it back.
- Enough light. Painting areas white and mirrors might be useful in the darker months. Plants need light to help photosynthesis and produce the energy they need to grow and develop. Some need more than others. A well lit windowsill and a seed tray might be all you need to get started.
- Enough heat. Plants when starting from seed generally need a temperature trigger to promote growth from dormancy. Some other seeds are triggered by colder temperatures so need the trigger of a fridge to get things started. Most vegetables and fruit are started in the Spring so benefit from the trigger of warmth. If you don't want to use seed trays, then home made plant pots made from tin

cans or yoghurt pots with drainage holes in the bases and sat on lids and inside plastic bag tents on a windowsill will do the trick to kick things off on the windowsill. Spinach and winter garlic and onions however, do well starting late Autumn.

- Your list of plants that you want to grow, with a plan of where you think they might grow best in your space, and what times of year they will be producing.
- Ways to access water. Put the containers where they can be watered by you initially and later, by the rain.
- Growing medium. Ok if you are starting indoors, you want a seed starter mix, and a potting mix for the second stage. You can buy these, but it is cheaper and easy to make, and will be able to be reused. Seed starter mixes need to be well draining, moisture retentive and easy for seeds to send roots and shoots through. Use one part coir or leaf mould, one part compost and 1 part organic perlite or sand. This mixed together makes a well draining, yet water retentive mix perfect for starting seeds and should we less likely to damp off than just compost. Clearly coir is sustainable but travels a long way if you are getting this in Europe, so leaf mould might be a more favoured ingredient, and you can easily make it yourself. I haven't mentioned vermiculite as an ingredient because it is not sustainable although it is organic and I love the stuff.
- When it comes to potting on, make the mix again but add two parts coir or leaf mould and two parts compost to one part perlite or horticultural sand.

Edible plants needs

Begin with a few plants and build up as you gain more confidence. I'll cover a few basics here to start. I've made recommendations at the end of the book if you want to research and take things further. The veggies are listed as Brassicas, roots and legumes, which is the basis for rotation when planning how to move veggies each year so as to avoid pest build up and soil depletion. They are hungry and required to produce so they need feeding.

Veg

Plant rotation group/ Family : Brassica/

Plant type and cultivar : Kale 'Nero Di Toscana'

Sowing seed/bulb planting and onwards: Sow thinly indoors March. April - May outdoors. Pot on to pots at least 25cm x 25cm. If in a planting bed then 45cm between each plant. They will need feeding.

Plant rotation group/ Family : Brassica/

Plant type and cultivar Radish 'Scarlet Globe'

Sowing seed/bulb planting and onwards: Sow March till August thinly in pots at least 15cm x 15cm you could grow maybe 4 in this sized pot. They need space to grow; 2 seeds per hole and remove the weaker germinating seeds after no more than 3 days. If sown in a bed prick out to 10cm between each plant.They should be ready in 1 month. They don't need feeding

Plant rotation group/ Family: Brassica

Plant type and cultivar: Wild Rocket

Sowing seed/bulb planting and onwards: Sow indoors March, outdoors April - August. Direct sow thinly in pots at least 25cm x

25cm with a plastic bag tent every 2 weeks for constant supply and simply remove the tent when acclimatised to outdoors. Thin plants out to 20cm inbetween if you want individual plants to reach their potential. Can grow into later months if protected. Very generous crop

Plant rotation group/ Family: Roots/Allium

Plant type and cultivar: Garlic 'Wight Christo'

Sowing seed/bulb planting and onwards: Plant in Autumn, or in Spring after the last frost. Each clove pointing upwards 3cm deep 15cm apart, So if you have 20cm x 20cm pots you could plant 1 per pot. If in a bed plant 15cm apart and 45cm between rows. They love the sun, good drainage and do well to be fed.

Plant rotation group/ Family: Legumes

Plant type and cultivar: Dwarf french beans 'Purple Queen'

Sowing seed/bulb planting and onwards: Sow April indoors and plant out after the last frost. Sow direct outside June onwards 2 beans per hole only a little deeper than the bean itself, 15cm apart. They don't need staking. Cut off the beans as soon as they are ready to encourage more. These guys love to feed. Set up another pot as soon as one is growing for a continuous supply.

Plant rotation group/ Family: Roots/ Solanacea

Plant type and cultivar: Potato 'Swift' First early

Sowing seed/bulb planting and onwards: Potato bags/ tubs are a simple way to plant and harvest. Find one approx 30 - 40 litres. Make sure it has holes in the base for drainage and put in 10cm compost. Then lay out 4 chitting potatoes and cover with 10cm compost and water. Repeat compost layers as the plants continue to grow, always leaving the growing tips showing until the container is full. Water regularly so well watered without being soggy. Harvest when the plants have flowered and died back.

Plant rotation group/ Family: Looseleaf lettuce / cut and come again is generally the Aster family. Can fit in anywhere. Colourful and tasty.

Plant type and cultivar: Cut and come again lettuce. Any mix.

Sowing seed/bulb planting and onwards: The container can be broad and as shallow as 15cm as long as watered regularly. Sow across the container, cover lightly with compost mix, and cover with a plastic tent for early sowings from Feb onwards until frosts finish. Some seed mixes can be cut up to 4 times before finished. Resow for continuous growing.

Plant rotation group/ Family: Amaranthus family. Can fit in anywhere

Plant type and cultivar: Spinach. Perpetual

Sowing seed/bulb planting and onwards: Spinach can be sown Under protection from Feb in Spring then Mar- May, or Autumn Aug - Sep, direct into containers at least 25cm x 25cm thinly. Thin again to 8cm apart when the seedlings are big enough to handle. Feed and water well. Pick off any slugs. Give a little shade in summer and sun and protection in winter. There are summer and winter types too.

Fruit

Family of fruit: Rosacea; Strawberry

Sowing/planting: Get a mixed pack from a good supplier (see list at end), to span the season. Otherwise get a good standard strawberry like 'Cambridge Favourite'. If you can, get plants in late Summer/ Autumn in prep for the following year. They like to be spaced 30cm x 75cm apart if in a bed, and so if you get a pot make it large enough to accommodate a few plants. They like a lot of food, water, drainage and sun from Spring time onwards. Once a week, and putting some extra feed in the soil when planting will help. Using a mulch like straw really helps hold in the mixture and protect the fruit from splash back.

Family of fruit: Rosaceae; Malus; eating apple, Pyrus, pear and Prunus Plum, Desert Apple, 'Falstaff', Pear 'Concorde' and Plum 'Victoria' On dwarf rooting stock as container cordon collection. See supplier list at end for ideas.

Sowing/planting: Plant in containers as vertical cordons to reach 1.8m height max. Prune to retain side lateral shape. If planted in a bed can be put as close as 60 - 90 cm apart. 50cm diameter pots 50-60 litres are good.

Square foot gardening and principles of rotation

This is an awesome way of maximising space. The idea is that in building a frame 4ft x 4ft with a depth of 12 inches and an internal grid to create a 4 x 4 layout, filled with compost we then put one crop per square. Planning the taller crops to go at the back of the bed and being in a sunny spot with shorter crops at the front. Most squares might be planted with one plant. Medium plants might have 4 per square, (including Swiss chard, parsley, basil and a number of other leafy greens, medium/small might have 9 plants per square, (peas, beetroot, large turnips, parsnips, kohlrabi and spinach.) Each of your seeds or seedlings will be placed four inches apart.

Photo by Kate Laine on Unsplash

Watering ; so everything needs watering but different amounts. When we have seedlings to water we use a spray gun and little amounts, and with bigger plants in the Summer we have water cans and big saucers underneath. It is all about noticing what is required. Sometimes we can check most accurately by sticking our fingers in the soil to check if it is dry or wet or somewhere in between which is what we are looking for. Too wet and the plants can't access oxygen via the roots. Too dry and they will be thirsty. You might also notice that rain water has a much better effect on plant growth than water from the tap. This is because rain water is soft water so it doesn't overwhelm plants with lots of excess minerals or additives that might be found in tap water.

Rainwater harvesting from an allotment greenhouse

Rainwater harvesting

Rainwater harvesting is something we can all do. Not only are we collecting water from a direct and natural source from rain to water our plants, we are saving on our water bills too. It's a win win! Even just placing a pot outdoors to catch the rain helps. If you have space to set up a water butt from guttering off any building then go for it. Water butts come in all sizes and shapes, and can be connected to each other at the bottom or the top in a line to maximise water storage capacity. Have a look at the end of the book here for some supplier ideas.

Feeding

Feeding. From the point of time after potting on your plants from growing their second pair of leaves, (which signifies the point when they are beginning to access their energy from the immediate environment rather than the seed they arrived in), your plants will need feeding. Depending on your time available, you might like to make or buy your plant food. I use different foods according to the environment and requirement of a space. I really like to make my own, and sometimes I buy them. If I have a space that needs fairly established plants to be fed outdoors, I might use a bought mix of rock dust or calcified seaweed or kelp powder with or without bone meal and blood fish and bone.

When planting, cutting back, dividing, or doing seasonal care I might use this same mix plus mycorrhizal to help establish root systems.

Nettle Photo by Les Argonautes on Unsplash

If I have nettle and comfrey growing in the space, and a container I can use, I might cut back the comfrey and nettle and soak them in a lidded container of water and then use the water a few weeks later to feed my plants.

Sometimes I get a seaweed plant food liquid for plants indoors or outdoors as a feed to be diluted in a watering can during a growing season.

Here are some recipes for making your own, and please see some product listings at the end of the book for ideas too.

You can chop up banana peel into chunks, half fill a jar and top up with warm water overnight and use the water a day later to water house plants. There is lots of Potassium in the skin which leeches into the water to feed the plants.

Soaking banana peel to make plant fertiliser

I do all of the above according to the requirements of a growing space.

Nettle and Comfrey Plant Feed

Find a container to use for your Plant food brew. Harvest comfrey and young nettle together if you can. Half fill your container with the leaves and fill up the container to the top with water and put the lid on. Within a couple of weeks the plant materials will be breaking down into the water and fermenting into a plant food. It will smell as the process of fermentation produces the smell. If the water looks like a weak tea, then that is the perfect plant food! If you want a less stinky plant food, then put the leaves in a bucket with a lid, and after maybe a month you will have a dark liquid at the bottom of the container that can be added to water at point of watering.

Mulching

When our plants are in their final position in containers or the ground they can all benefit by mulching. All this means is we cover the ground that is being used for growing. The purpose of covering the ground is to slow evaporation of moisture, weed growth and loss of nutrients and in some cases even build the soil; it's a win win and a lot of mulch materials are free recyclables. Here is a list of mulches you might like to use:

Leaves Photo by Annie Spratt on Unsplash

- Cardboard. You can literally cut a cardboard collar and put on the soil surface
- Newspaper. I'd use dampened layers
- Wool packing insulation. Cut as a plant collar. This can also help deter slugs and snails
- Strulch. A straw mulch feeds the soil, deters pests and helps hold moisture and nutrients
- Composted bark
- Home made compost
- Leaves; composted or not
- Bark chip; this is best on big established plants with deep roots
- Comfrey leaves; breaking down and feeding the soil
- Fresh straw or hay
- Wood shavings
- Coir processed into a compost
- Cut herbs /forage
- Re-use of crop harvest residues local to you, (corn, rice husk, cotton gin, vines, cut/ chopped plants).
- Green living mulches. Low growing, often nitrogen fixing ground cover plants like Clover.
- Landscape fabric. There are increasing eco fabrics and mats made from recycled and slowly composting materials; quite often crop waste.
- There are plastic based non eco landscape fabrics and mats, which if looked after well can last ages, but eventually will hit the bin and also the landfill. I would advise that if you really have to use plastic based non composting fabrics, cut them as you need and literally hem the raw edges as best you can to avoid shredding by weather and wild animals. They last a lot longer that way.

- Stones on top of a mat mulch helps keep down weeds and keep in moisture and nutrients. Because of the 'bittiness' of it, it will take time to remove it if you want to access the soil underneath. Pick stones larger than 20mm if you really want to use them, (anything smaller cats like too much). Best use for a stone mulch I think is of varied sizes on pots or ground you are treating like a sea/alpine-scape and doesn't need any mat underneath.

Clover Photo by Ankur Dutta on Unsplash

Planting and planning for wildlife

We need pollinators and predators to help us manage and be part of our biodiversity both in immediate and distant environments. By thinking on Companion planting, bug hotels, watering stations, healthy soil building, wintering stations, chemical free pest management and other methods like this we can help attract and support wildlife as well as look after our Sanctuary in a sustainable way. Bug hotels can in the smallest fashion be a mini wall mounted bee hotel, or an upturned pot filled with leaves and compost with easy access. What can your space accommodate, and who do you want to visit? A water station can be a large water and stone filled plant saucer at ground height and or a recycled plastic bottle hanging from a hook or a branch.

Mini bug hotel Photo by Mika Baumeister on Unsplash

Overcoming pitfalls; what can go wrong and why try again.

Even when we have looked, thought, made plans and added as we have gone along we can come up against issues. Don't let them deter you. Look to see why they happened and make a tiny shift in your method to overcome them. It is common to be taken by surprise by a sudden weather change either very hot or cold or wet or dry ; especially at the change of the season and more so as we have additional factors at play.

If you sowed the seeds and they were damped off from being too wet, lift the bag or lid off a little every day to check air flow, look at dampening the seed soil mix slightly less and maybe sprinkle with cinnamon powder to stop mould.

If you transferred seedlings and they died from a too powerful sun, then sow more and look at transferring them on a grey cooler day, or later in the day in a slightly less sunny position.

If you have been outnumbered by slugs and snails, invite the birds with water stations to help and try organic slug and snail pellets in small quantities.

If you have an aphid or other small infestation, try the washing off technique and pest deterrent recipe plus more companion plants to attract predators.

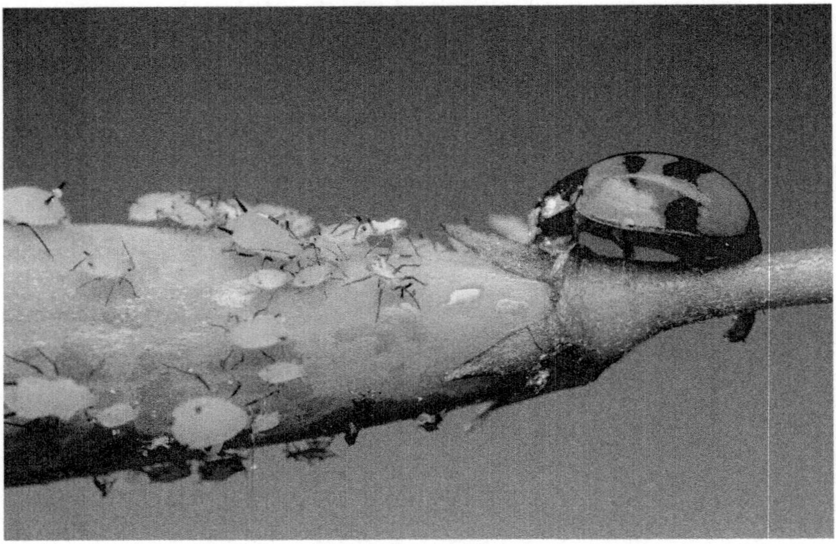

Photo by Henry Lai on Unsplash

It is small tweaks that make the differences. Your second try will no doubt be a winner.

Harvesting and storing

Picking the fruits/veg/herbs of your labours is sooo satisfying. I think the reason I love Kale and Chard so much is that you can just keep on picking for ages. Try picking leaves and herbs just as you need them, but if picking ahead of time, wrap in a damp cloth or paper and store in the fridge for a few days before use.

People used to use 'root cellars' to store root veg. If short on space either leave them in the ground till just before you need them, or bury them in a bucket of damp sand and straw with a lid, kept in a cooler shady spot and use as needed.

Apples and pears do well for being kept in dry temperature stable well aerated conditions.

Photo by Rebecca Matthews on Unsplash

Soft fruits are great fresh, frozen, or bottled in syrups. Tomatoes can be canned, bottled, made into sauces and bottled or dried in slices.

Saving seed

Seed can be easily saved. Cucumbers/ courgette/tomatoes/pumpkins can literally have their pips spread out on a kitchen paper towel, air dried, labelled and saved in a folded paper envelope for the following year. Chard, amaranths, carrot, and herbs can be cut and hung upside down with a paper bag over the top to collect seed. After this the seeds can be collected and stored in a temperature stable environment in a paper envelope. Biscuit tins in dry dark cupboards will do. Try and use the seed the following year to keep a live source of seeds and avoid accumulating seeds with a reducing germination rate.

Photo by Joshua Lanzarini on Unsplash

Can we grow all year round? How?

By looking at what space we have available with sun all the year round, and looking at what plants like growing through winter, (winter onion, garlic, cabbage, some hardy lettuce), for instance), and where we might be able to cover a crop using fleece layers, we can easily grow food all the year round, on any scale. I would highly recommend looking for the Cook's planning calendar by HDRA/ Garden Organic, or another reputable source.

Sprouting

Another way of growing through the year is by getting into growing sprouted seeds. Lots of seeds can be sprouted and eaten; alfalfa, mung beans, chives, fenugreek, red clover, adzuki, lentil, mustard, black sunflower, soybean, kale, radish, peas.

Use seeds that are meant for eating directly rather than sowing, and this will avoid dealing with seeds that have been coated with inedible inorganic coatings purposed for planting.

You grow the sprouts in either a stacking seed sprouter device or a jar and use a cotton and rubber band lid to allow air movement.

Method

Soak enough seeds to cover the base of your jar/ sprouter lightly overnight, then drain and spread. Put the stacker lid or jar cotton in place and put in a light window sill or shelf. Rinse the seeds twice a day. After a few days, (slightly longer in winter), you will have edible sprouts. They can be kept in the fridge for a few days.

Buckwheat and lentils in a sprouter day 1

Pests. Diseases. Seasons are a changin…….

Ok you've decided you want to grow some edibles in your space.

Using our senses and spending time outdoors can help us become more aware of how things change as much as stay the same.

Pests; start simple

So if you want to grow edible plants, the likelihood is that something else may have those plants on the menu too. There are natural techniques we can deploy to deter the pests, break the feeding and breeding cycle, and boost the immunity of the plants so that they can overcome any pest loading pathogens that might otherwise weaken their systems.

Firstly I'd recommend washing off as many critters above/ below ground on your plants first and consider changing the soil.

Secondly, consider when planning your planting to include herbs and flowers and companion plants that are known to add value to biodiversity, deter pests and increase natural predators by offering another supply of pollen and nectar as well as possibly exude scent and oils that help improve the chances of your plants and you thriving.

Companion Plants

Companion plants are plants which can feed and attract beneficial insects, or and may also deter pests you don't want. Some are considered as wholly beneficial e.g. if thinking in terms of pollination, like nasturtiums and calendula. Others might be in relation directly to supporting certain plants. Equally, there are some plants which don't make the best neighbours because they can share certain pests and diseases.

The list for fruit and veg companion planting is extensive. I would suggest looking on Wikipedia for a more comprehensive list (6).

Here is a simple list that you might find useful for small spaces;

- Mints. Smells great, and are very quick to grow and have a tendency to take over, so keep in their own pot next to potatoes, brassicas, carrots, lettuce, tomatoes and marigolds.
- Calendula. Great source of pollen throughout the growing season, so attractive to pollinators. Deters some pests eg. asparagus beetle and soil nematode. May also attract slugs. So great for asparagus and tomatoes but maybe not for potatoes.
- Tagetes. (T citriodora, T patula, T erecta, T minuta). Great at feeding pollinators pollen and nectar and therefore attract beneficial insects. I don't know any plants which are suppressed by this companion.
- Nasturtium. Attracts beneficial insects and also traps pest insects that would otherwise attack your crops. It also has edible leaves, flowers and seeds.
- Alliums grow well with carrots, brassicas, tomatoes, peppers, potato and fruit trees, but not beans and peas.

I really like to put at least three lemon scented herbs in close proximity as early in the year as possible, (lemon balm, lemon marigold, lemon mint, are earlier, lemon grass, lemon verbena are later), plus any early flowering herbs and cultivated edible wild flowers, so as to encourage and benefit pollinators and insects that may hunt down the aphids. There is a reason for this. Not only will these beneficial insects be able to sustain and multiply and suppress the expansion of detrimental pests like aphids, but they also help stop the spread of plant diseases carried by the pests. Every Spring I watch a Cherry and Silver Birch come into leaf as their sap rises. Then the aphids come to feast, and I try to encourage the beneficial insects so they can calm down the aphid infestations before the appearance of leaf curl on the Cherry tree. There is another anomaly I don't interfere with which is that the bumble and honey bees harvest the aphid nectar but that is the brilliance of nature!

Carrots help allium, beans, lettuce, leeks, tomatoes, but don't do well with dill, parsnip and radish.

Also, some beneficial plants that offer pollen for pollinators might be best grown close by but not in the same containers as your edibles as they might exude chemicals that actually keep other plants from growing to their full potential. Fennel is a good example of this.

Nettle and Comfrey are also great food plants for pollinators, and make great fertiliser for growing plants, but due to their potential size at their largest in a season, they should be grown nearby but not in the same container or patch as your edibles.

Some pest deterrent sprays you might see on the shelf in a shop are usually toxic to people and pets. So why would you want to use them on food plants?

to make and apply a home made pest deterrent organic spray;

Basic Pest Deterrent Spray Recipe

- 1 litre warm water
- 1 bulb garlic pulped
- 1 dessert spoon cayenne
- 100ml liquid seaweed feed
- 50ml washing up liquid
- 50ml cooking oil

Process the garlic and cayenne with half the water, soap and oil and add the rest of the water. Steep for 12 hours, strain and pop into a spray bottle.

Planning for your next growing success

If you keep ideas, notes, sketches, photos, seeds and plans during your time experimenting growing, you will be easily be able to plan for what you want to do the next year, with adjustments to meet your experience, requirements and imagination.

Rotating your veggies will only be a small part of it. You will most likely have strong ideas about how you could use your space next year.

Photo by Markus Spiske on Unsplash

Conclusion

I hope you found this book fun and helpful to help kickstart/vitalise your journey into empowering, restorative ideas to get you started growing edible plants in small urban spaces sustainably. I really believe we can rebuild and renew vitality in so many complex ways in our Sanctuaries and add so much value to spaces and our lives.

I would really appreciate your review on Amazon so look forward to seeing your comments there; let me know how the book helped you, and maybe which direction you are headed next!

Happy growing,

Sarah

5

Resources

(1). Retrieved October 18, 2022, from https://www.researchgate.net/figure/The-new-general-plan-of-Ur-drawn-up-by-F-Ghio-1-City-Wall-2-North-Harbour-3_fig12_258386554

(2). London's Alleys: Old Fish Street Hill, EC4. (2022, July 16). ianVisits. Retrieved October 18, 2022, from https://www.ianvisits.co.uk/articles/londons-alleys-old-fish-street-hill-ec4-56087/

(3). Wikipedia contributors. (2022e, September 30). Organopónicos. Wikipedia. Retrieved October 18, 2022, from https://en.wikipedia.org/wiki/Organop%C3%B3nicos

(4). Adams, B. (2019, November 5). In Detroit, A New Type of Agricultural Neighborhood Has Emerged. YES! Magazine. Retrieved October 18, 2022, from https://www.yesmagazine.org/social-justice/2019/11/05/food-community-detroit-garden-agriculture

(5). Harrison, J. Y. M. (2022, February 17). The Urban Farms Growing Community in Vacant Chicago Lots. Civil Eats. Retrieved October 18, 2022, from https://civileats.com/2022/02/18/the-urban-farms-growing-community-in-vacant-chicago-lots/

(6). Wikipedia contributors. (2022a, August 27). List of companion plants. Wikipedia. Retrieved October 18, 2022, from https://en.wikipedia.org/wiki/List_of_companion_plants

Definitions as currently understood/negotiated

Huerto - small organic family run gardens - Retrieved October 18, 2022, from https://www.collinsdictionary.com/dictionary/spanish-english/huerto

Organoponico - larger organic gardens run by many people as cooperatives by stakeholders. Wikipedia contributors. (2022c, September 30). Organopónicos. Wikipedia. Retrieved October 18, 2022, from https://en.wikipedia.org/wiki/Organop%C3%B3nicos

Agroecology - The science, movement or practise of alternative agriculture. Wikipedia contributors. (2022a, July 7). Agroecology. Wikipedia. Retrieved October 18, 2022, from https://en.wikipedia.org/wiki/Agroecology

Urban Ecology - The practice and study of achieving a balance between humans and the natural environment. Wikipedia contributors. (2022e, October 11). Urban ecology. Wikipedia. Retrieved October 18, 2022, from https://en.wikipedia.org/wiki/Urban_ecology

Regenerative Agriculture - Working towards a sustainable whole in agriculture. Wikipedia contributors. (n.d.). Regenerative agricultur - Wikipedia. Retrieved October 18, 2022, from https://en.wikipedia.org/wiki/Regenerative_agricultur

Agri hood means agricultural neighbourhood - check it out on wikipedia; Wikipedia contributors. (2022a, March 8). Agrihood. Wikipedia. Retrieved October 18, 2022, from https://en.wikipedia.org/wiki/Agrihood

Suppliers

Fruit trees - Pomona fruit - https://www.pomonafruits.co.uk/

Brogdale - https://brogdalecollections.org/

Heritage seeds - Realseeds - https://www.realseeds.co.uk/

HDRA Heritage seed library - https://www.gardenorganic.org.uk/hsl

Organic Feeds - Vitax Calcified Seaweed https://amzn.eu/d/8YQkPpk

Water butts - https://amzn.eu/d/7MAajqW

Eco mats; https://gardenersupplies.co.uk/ecomatt-bio-biodegradable-weed-fabric-mat/?sku=150WW2623&utm_source=google&utm_medium=cpc&utm_campaign=all-products&gclid=Cj0KCQjwnP-ZBhDiARIsAH3FSRff_gHSo2VbcBICzn7_DmZHofhM8yKsi7GX-y7eRcHcm0qJSPRUkhQaAtFhEALw_wcB

About the Author

I have loved hanging out with, exploring natural environments and growing plants since I was a very small person. I still do and I adore that I still can learn so much more and hopefully help inspire people of all ages that they have nothing to fear from engaging with, enjoying, exploring and devising their own path into this jungle sustainably no matter what space is available.

You can connect with me on:

- http://www.sarahnewtongardendesign.com
- https://twitter.com/newtonsarah
- https://www.facebook.com/people/Sarah-Newton-Garden-Design/100039975646610

Subscribe to my newsletter:

- https://sarahnewtongardendesign.com